## The Praise Literary Collection
# TESTIMONIALS

Unmerited Favor and Divine Provision

Copyright© 2016 Angel Miller Barrino, Angel B. Inspired Inc.

Unless otherwise indicated all scripture references are from the King James Version, New International Version, English Standard Versions of the Bible, used by permission. Scripture quotations are from the ESV® Bible (The Holy Bible, English Standard Version®), copyright © 2001 by Crossway, a publishing ministry of Good News Publishers. Used by permission. All rights reserved.

THE HOLY BIBLE, NEW INTERNATIONAL VERSION® NIV®
Copyright © 1973, 1978, 1984 by International Bible Society®
Used by permission. All rights reserved worldwide.

All rights reserved. No part of this book may be reproduced (except by the co-authors), stored in any electronic system, or transmitted in any form by any means, without written permission from the publisher and primary author, except for use of brief quotations in reviews. The publisher gives express permission for each author to use their testimonials in reviews, promotions but not to be reproduced in any other publication. Individual author contact information is provided within each chapter.

**ISBN: 978-0-9861335-8-9**

Printed In USA

## TABLE OF CONTENTS

SPECIAL DEDICATION ........................................................................... 4
ACKNOWLEDGEMENTS ........................................................................ 5
FOREWORD ............................................................................................ 6
INTRODUCTION ................................................................................... 10
HOW I GOT OVER ................................................................................ 13
THE BLESSING OF FAVOR .................................................................. 18
ALMOST NO MOTHER ........................................................................ 23
HE LOVES ME ....................................................................................... 30
UNMERITED FAVOR: A HEALING KEY ............................................ 39
WALKING IN FANTASTIC FAVOR ..................................................... 45
LEVI'S TESTIMONY .............................................................................. 51
WHERE DO I BEGIN? ........................................................................... 56
FROM A CRASH TO A CAUSE ............................................................ 63
UNMERITED FAVOR & DIVINE PROVISION OF THE FIRST KIND ...... 68
FAITH AND FAVOR .............................................................................. 75

## SPECIAL DEDICATION

This book is in honor of my Paternal Grandparents: Paul and Louise Miller; my aunts & uncles: Mary Minor, Eddie Minor, Geraldine Moore, Clementine Jones, Isaiah Miller, Daisy Miller, Steve Miller, James Miller, Ezekiel Miller; and dear cousins who have departed this earthly existence. The love they shared with me, along with the love and support of those who are still with me, propels me forward with divine purpose, passion and faith.

Unmerited Favor & Divine Provision is also dedicated to those who understand the heartbeat of the Father; His provision and His desire for His children to live an abundant life. Through worship and honor of Him this book project was birthed. From many challenges we have become victorious and better worshippers of Him, recognizing Him as Shepherd, Father, Provider, Protector, Savior and Sovereign.

## ACKNOWLEDGEMENTS

I am eternally grateful and thankful for the goodness, mercy and favor Abba Father bestows upon my life; His unfailing love and kindness towards me is immeasurable. Without Him I would be nothing.

**To the woman who is my sister-friend and business bestie, Elder Desireé Harris-Bonner**: I love you and I am so grateful for our hearts and spirits being knitted together spiritually to bring forth anointed and powerful projects which bless the world. Thank you so much for believing in me and this vision.

**To each co-author and contributing author:** Thank you for sharing your gift of writing, which has come alive through these pages. Your life messages are being shared with many and I am honored you believed enough in this project to present them here.

**To my family and friends:** Thank you for your love and support which helps me endure. For every season of my life many of you have walked with me – Abba Father has blessed me with the gifts of close friendships, family and mentors who encourage, inspire, motivate and propel me higher.

**To the readers:** You make writing and publishing worth it. Thank you.

# FOREWORD

By Bishop Garland Heggie and Ladie Sarah Grace

*Bishop Garland Heggie*

When people are sick, a doctor will, many times, prescribe some type of medical regimen to soothe the symptoms and combat the disease. If anyone is sick or broken, financially discouraged, or are dealing with any type of trial or trauma, trouble, or tribulation, I would prescribe to them this book, *"Testify"*.

It is rich in power, because of the sincerity and authenticity of the testimonies within its covers. The Word of God states, that when Satan warred against Heaven and Michael and his angels were dispatched to contend in battle, one of the ways they prevailed, was by the "word of their testimony".

This reveals the potency of these stories of survival and success from the test and storms the writers have experienced. In a fight with the devil, they were able to disarm him with a testimony. They were able to wound him with a testimony. They were able to hold off his advances with a testimony. They experienced victory, because of a testimony.

And no matter what your situation or affliction, it is coming from the same enemy. So, there is no need to try and reinvent the wheel. The same manner the angels were able to be victorious over the devil, is the same way you can have victory over him now.

God inspired our Angel (Barrino) to publish this book full of testimonies to add to our arsenal, since the weapons of our warfare are not carnal, to assist us in winning our own individual wars. Many of my personal victories have been the result of someone else's testimony; therefore, I encourage you to be empowered and inspired by those brave enough to "testify" in the pages of this book, and from their testimonies, you will be the one left standing after the dust settles from the fight you are presently in. I then encourage you to testify, so someone else can be armed for their battle, by the word of your testimony.

Let this book become the beginning of a never-ending series of *yoke breaking, burden removing,* and *glory provoking* testimonies.

*Bishop Garland Heggie*
Sr. Pastor | Community Fellowship Christian Church

\*\*\*

*Ladie Sarah Grace*

It is one thing to preach and teach from Psalm 23, better known as the "Shepherd's Psalm", but it's a completely different thing to live it. Though I had been preaching for years prior to becoming divorced and left to be the sole parent and provider for the seven children awarded to my now severed union, the words of this passage jumped out of the book and manifested in my life in a way that I could go from saying "I believe" to "I know."

Within the first several months following the finalization of my divorce, I found myself exhausted of all savings, void of any income, without a penny of child support, and constantly being sent through inexhaustible red tape in my quest for government assistance. I had faced the difficulty of late rent, mortgage or utility payments, car payments, and the like throughout life, but there was never a time that I didn't know how I would be able to afford food or shelter altogether, until then.

However, just when it looked like there were no options, no open doors, and no means for my family to avoid homelessness and hunger, God showed up and showed out, and hasn't stopped yet.

For the last five years, I have experienced the miraculous in the area of provision. Homes and a vehicle I didn't qualify for by natural standards, are at the top of my list of major breakthroughs in the area of provision; but my list is extensive, even to include things like birthdays and holidays, where I could not do the things for my children that I wanted to, and I watched Him do what only He could do.

I have also seen God do with favor, what money in and of itself cannot. God can put you in the right place, at the right time, with the right people, to meet the exact need! God's favor can provide for your needs and your desires physically, financially and even emotionally, when the dam of your emotions seems to have broken through stress… God's favor will come and offer you a release from your stress. I have even been on all expense paid retreats and conferences, which were huge catalysts to God rebuilding my soul and renewing my countenance.

I am here to tell you today that I don't only believe, but rather that I KNOW, that the Lord IS my Shepherd and I have experienced His supernatural favor and provision in many areas of my life, and it is His will for you that are reading this book, to experience it too. I encourage you to open up your heart, stir up your expectation, and get ready for elevation in your belief system concerning supernatural favor and provision.

*Ladie Sarah Grace*
Minister | Author | Visionary

# INTRODUCTION

Trusting God is not easy.

In fact, trusting Him is one of the hardest things to do. Having faith in the unseen and eternal seems illogical for many people; yet for others, it seems to be a way of life.

*Unmerited Favor and Divine Provision* represents the unseen, supernatural, manifested and resurrected power of Abba Father through the lives of a handpicked few. The collection is a compilation of love letters describing the preemptive nature and sovereignty of our Daddy God. These stories depict His love, character, favor; His presence, peace, protection, and most of all, His provision.

The anointing, His burden-removing and yoke-destroying power, resonates through the words written on these pages, from the lives of His children who courageously share their testimonies in this great work. Be blessed by the transparent journey each author displays.

May your life be changed, and may the Father be glorified, as you discover a deeper connection with Him through these pages.

We love you and we are praying for you.

*Angel B. & the Unmerited Favor Team*

*And they overcame him by the blood of the Lamb, and by the word of their testimony; and they loved not their lives unto the death.*

*~Revelations 12:11*

## HOW I GOT OVER
### ELDER D.H.BONNER

I looked in the mirror the other day, and gazing right back at me, was a face I easily recognized; having awakened to encounter her image each morning for slightly more than 50 years.

She wore her hair the same way I did.

She possessed the same button-sized nose, full lips, and deeply brown skin that I did.

And, she watched me with the same level of intensity and mindfulness with which I peered at her.

When I smiled, she beamed back at me, with an equally toothy grin. She even had a birthmark on her face in the exact same spot I did.

So, there was no surprise for me to see her that morning; however, this time, I noticed something... something different. The reflection that peered back at me in that moment gave me the impression that she was a bit older, a little wiser, and definitely more experienced than I last remembered.

Behind her gentle, maturing eyes, it appeared as if she held a secret... a knowing beyond what was expected.

I paused for a moment, and because I wanted to know more, I opened my mouth and asked, *"Self?"*

Self said, *"Huh?"*

*What's going on with you? Why do you look different this morning?"*

She slowly smiled and said, *"I finally figured it out."*

Hmmm... she had my full attention.

*"Figured what out?"* I asked.

She didn't answer right away, so I leaned in closer, and rested my hands on the countertop for balance. I didn't want to miss one word.

After a couple of breaths, she parted her lips and whispered, *"I figured out how we got over."*

What? What is she talking about?

As I attempted to wrap my mind around the answer to a question I just now was able to acknowledge I had, she continued to share her thoughts. *"I know you've been wondering. Trying to figure out how you got from there to here. How you've been able to get up each and every morning, still placing one foot in front of the other, when all you want to do is stay in bed with the covers over your head; not knowing how you're going to make it through another day, or another week, another month; let alone another year.*

*I know how you've been wondering where the money is going to come from to keep a roof over your head and stop the disconnect notices from being simple warnings to becoming reality.*

*And, I know you've been wondering whether you've truly been operating in faith all this time, or if you've been pushing the boundaries of foolishness!*

I began preparing my mouth to ask her, how it was possible that she could know all of this, when I remembered who I was talking to.

So, I chose instead to meditate on all that had passed over the past five decades of my life. And, while continuing to keep my eyes fastened upon those being reflected back at me, I saw past events, playing like a film strip, just beyond the beautiful flicks of medium to light brown resonating in a pool of the slightly aging whites of her eyes.

The short film began with the abusive husband, the miscarriage, the suicidal thoughts, the rejection, and the two divorces; concluding with a Chapter 13 bankruptcy, in which I paid off in excess of $100K of debt, within four and half years. Then, as soon as that was completed, being laid off from a high-level corporate job, before I could even get back on my feet and rebuild my financial reserves; only to be followed by the aftermath of losing my cars, home, material possessions, and some very key relationships in my life.

The image looking back at me began to tear up... and then openly cry.

Pulling a tissue from the box on the vanity, I asked her, *"Why are you crying? I thought you were healed of all that emotional pain."*

*"I am..."*

*"Then, why the tears?"* I asked, gently wiping them away, even as they were freely flowing down her cheek.

*"Because, I realize that if it had not been..."*

My voice joined hers. *"For the Lord on my side..."*

We both laughed out loud!

And, in unison, we started to sing.

> *How I got over*
> *How did I make it over?*
> *You know my soul look back and wonder*
> *How did I make it over?*[1]

I took one long, last look in the mirror, at that woman who had endured, yet triumphed over so much, and nodded. Walking out of the room, I turned off the light, grateful that I no longer have to wonder how I got over...

It was His Unmerited Favor and Divine Provision.

---

[1] From *"How I Got Over"*, by Mahalia Jackson

**Elder Desireé Harris-Bonner** is an International award-winning Vocalist and formally trained Percussionist, who operates in the Body of Christ as a Psalmist. And, through the ministry of Music and the Word, she is anointed to provoke an atmosphere of worship, where God's presence can be felt and realized; hearts opened to His Holy Spirit, and lives drawn to Him.

She has released two Sacred Music CD's; "The Psalmist... Volume One" & "The Psalmist... Volume Two" and is currently in the studio, working on the Third Volume! A three-time Amazon bestselling Author, her first Book entitled *"The Heart of the Psalmist"* was published in November of 2012 and her second Book, *"To the Wounded Warrior"*, was released in 2014. She is also a contributor to the Anthology: *"Organized Obstacles"* with her story entitled "Unfinished: The Diary of a Psalmist".

Elder Bonner was graced to write the Foreword to the first **TESTIFY** compilation, *Testimonials,* and is currently penning both a Christian Novella and her next book entitled, *"Relational Miscarriages"*.

*"And He has put a new song in my mouth, a song of praise to our God. Many shall see and fear (revere and worship) and put their trust and confident reliance in the Lord."* ~Psalm 40:3

# THE BLESSING OF FAVOR
### EVANGELIST HIELEY RICHARDSON

*Wow! Where do I begin? When talking about God's favor, I get extremely excited!*

I'm grateful for the opportunity to share just a small portion of my experience of God's favor.

Having an understanding of what favor is will help you know how it operates. There is nothing magical or mystical about the favor of God; it is simply a special privilege afforded to those who have a relationship with Jesus Christ. The greatest gift of God's favor is having His presence in your life. When I gave my life to Christ, I began experiencing God's favor.

However, before I share my story, allow me to share a few things about God's divine favor: (1) we must understand that favor can't be bought with money and (2) it is a divine gift from God; therefore, everyone doesn't qualify for this special privilege.

Let's begin with me sharing a few examples of the blessings produced in my life as a result of having God's favor . . .

Two years ago, I worked a job and was told it would be closing. Management decided to let me go, forfeiting my opportunity to receive my severance pay; I was there just as long, if not longer than mostly everyone there. I must admit I was a little upset - not just because I was let go, but simply because I couldn't get what I knew belonged to me.

A couple of days later, I received a call from the manager asking if I could come back because someone had quit; they needed someone to temporarily help until the official closing day. My pride didn't want me to go back; however, I accepted the offer. Although I was only back for a short while, guess what? I received my severance pay . . . God reopened the door, just to give me what I was entitled to!

When God has something for you, nobody can stop it!

Additionally, while everyone was all worked up about not having a job and trying to find work, I was placed in another favorable situation. There was an insurance company two doors down from where I worked, and I went in one day to obtain a quote. This was only a few days after the announcement that my job would be closing. Upon receiving the quote, I was informed by the manager that he was looking for an office assistant.

Guess who got the job? Yep . . . Me! Can you say "Favor?"

When God's favor is on your life, He will take people down just to set you up, I am a witness. It's not that you rejoice in peoples' downfall, but when you walk upright before the Lord, favor is inevitable. God honors faithfulness! I started the job with the intent to have my insurance license within a couple of months. Well, two months turned into two years. The process became difficult and there were times when I felt like giving up. But because of the favor of God, I was able to finally pass that insurance exam and obtain my license.

Having God's favor does not mean that everything you set out to do will always be easy, but it will always produce favorable results. After five years of working for this company, I was notified that our office would be closing. During this time, my husband and I were in the process of purchasing a home. Our banker informed us that we needed about six hundred dollars, plus another two hundred for closing costs. One morning while sitting at my desk, my boss handed me a check for a thousand dollars as severance pay due to the office closing. This enabled us to have enough to take care of what was needed and some left over.

Can you say "Favor?"

While approaching the final day at my job, I was informed that another insurance agent down the street could use some extra help. I didn't even pursue the opportunity . . . the opportunity pursued me . . . Favor.

Upon a year and half at the new job, I began pursuing my dream of recording my first CD project. Due to the work involved with this project and feeling the call to do something more, I stepped out in faith and gave up my position. God provided everything I needed to fulfill my dream of recording my CD.

With being out of work and no income, bills were late. *"Lord what am I going to do,"* I asked. At church, one Sunday, not long after my Pastor preached a message entitled, "A one minute miracle," I said to myself, "I surely do need one." The very next day I went to the mailbox and there was a check for one thousand dollars. This was a real check sent from a loan company and the only thing I had to do was endorse and deposit it. What loan company gives a person a thousand dollar check without signing anything and with no job?

That's what God's favor will do!

I cashed that check quick, fast, and in a hurry! I was able to catch up on my bills, until the Lord opened another door of opportunity. God's favor will open doors no man can shut and place you in positions that you don't even qualify for. I have seen His hand of continued favor in my life and wouldn't trade it for anything in this world. So, when people ask me how I'm doing, I kindly and humbly say, *"I'm blessed and Hieley Favored!"*

That's my name! That's who I am! To God be all the glory!

**Evangelist Hieley Richardson** is a resident of Hollister NC and a member of the Haliwa Saponi Indian Tribe. She is married to Phillip Richardson Jr and they have two children, Jacob and Leah.

Hieley faithfully serves as Associate Minister at St. Gideon Baptist Church under the leadership of Pastor John R. Lee and was ordained in October 2016. She received her education in the Halifax County school system and graduated from Morgan Hill Community Adult School in Morgan Hill, CA. She later furthered her education at New Grace Bible Institute in Rocky Mount, NC where she obtained a degree in Theology.

She also holds a license in Property & Casualty. The reality of her dream came true in August 2013 when she recorded her first Gospel CD Project entitled "New Beginning."

Hieley is an anointed Preacher, Psalmist and Song Writer who has been blessed with the ability to lead others into the presence of the Lord. She draws her strength from her personal relationship with Christ and endeavors to lead others to a relationship with him as well. Her message is "If He did it for me, He can do it for you."

Hieley is a light and beacon of hope to all she comes in contact with. She loves to inspire others and see their life changed by the undying love of our Heavenly Father. She dedicates her life to serving others and being a blessing to the Kingdom of God. She believes that everyone has a purpose and strives to help people see themselves the way God sees them.

You may contact Evangelist Hieley Richardson via the social media platform of Facebook @ **Hieley Richardson** or **Gospel Artist Hieley Richardson.**

**Twitter @ HieleyFavored.**

**Email: hieleyrichardson@yahoo.com**

## ALMOST NO MOTHER
### LINDA D. WATTLEY

*"A mother; that presence in life letting you know you are not alone."*

"Good morning! Get up and get ready for school!" My father shouted as he went from my room to my brothers' rooms to begin our day. As I rolled out of bed to prepare for school, I took a quick look into my parents' room to see if my mom was still sleeping. She was not there.

That day, we went to school and returned home; still we did not see our mom. My father never mentioned her, and being so well disciplined and quiet with our communication with our parents, we never thought to ask where she was. All we know is days went into weeks, and weeks into months, with our not knowing where our mother was.

At night, I lay in my bed crying and in the fetal position, wanting to see and hear my mother's voice again. Finally, we heard our father talking to my grandmother, telling her she was not coming back home, and that he needed help in tending to me and my three brothers. We were cared for by friends and family members for a while, until one day, our lives were never the same. We ended up in a family merger; the stepfamily saga began forcing us to have a new mother, three step sisters, and brother. My brothers and I had to move forward without our own mother.

One day, while living in this new setting, our mother surfaced; begging for my father to give her back her children. However, we were forced to stay out of her reach or suffer the consequences. She came for us several times, until she was taken away in a paddy wagon. Years went by, and I forgot my mom's effort to get her children back. Instead, I was brainwashed to believe my mother did not want us and that she left us because she did not love us.

Eventually we were conditioned to accept this new family life. My stepmother became my mother; a woman who loved and cared for me. We had a very close relationship, even though it was not a healthy one. In some ways, I was very afraid of her, because when she did not get what she wanted out of you, she could say some horrible things and have violent tendencies.

Finally, my brothers and I were at the age where we could choose which parent we wanted to be with. Even though I was told my mother did not love or want me, I preferred to live with her than to stay under the care of my stepmother. We moved into my mother's home to learn she did not have enough money to provide for us on her low income.

We didn't care.

We did not want to leave, so we struggled day to day to have food and clothing. It was not long before we learned my mother had become an alcoholic and when she would drink, she was very mean, angry and violent. For some reason, I was the one she would attack on the regular. I remember one night, when she physically and verbally attacked me so badly I had to run out of the house, to save myself from potential death.

That night, I ran to my neighbor's house, because it was after midnight and my blouse was half torn off, hair all over my head and I had a huge black and swollen eye. When my neighbor opened the door, she thought I had been raped.

Though I was violently attacked by my mother, I couldn't forget what she was shouting. She kept shouting I loved my stepmother and that I didn't love her. I went to sleep that night finally with some kind of an idea why she was so mean to me.

For sure, we had to talk.

The next day, we talked. We learned, we both thought each of us hated each other based on how things appeared and what was said. My mother did not leave us; my father bullied her out of our lives. She couldn't take the beatings anymore and his extramarital affairs, so he revenged on her by threatening her and taking us away from her. That day she learned the times she told me to come to her when she attempted to take us with her, I couldn't run to her because I was threatened that great harm would come to me if I did. I also let her know I was told she didn't want or love me. We cried and apologized to each other and began rekindling our relationship.

It took years for us to trust and learn each other. It was not an easy journey, but eventually became a rewarding one as I went into adulthood. If we had not given each other a chance to know and love each other, I would have missed out on something wonderful. I have my mother in my life as my best friend, supporter, and grandmother to my children, as well as a renewed confidence in my walk, in life. I thank God every day for giving me such a wonderful mother.

Knowing how valuable a mother's presence is in a child's life, I take my role as a mother very seriously. Widowed at age twenty –eight with two sons, one four and the other two and a half years old, I made sure to be someone in their lives that is there for them, no matter what and will love them forever. You would think in life, life would agree, their father was killed instantly in a car accident, this woman is the only person they have be there for them. Right?

Well, let me tell you about life. In 1986, two years after my husband's tragic death in a car accident, I was rear-ended by a truck carrying 50 tons of asphalt that hit my 1976 Chevy Nova. Hands holding the steering wheel, and foot on the brake, my car was still moving through the intersection.

*"Ma'am are you alright?"* I heard, as I turned towards the voice, now looking at me with great concern.

*"I knew I was going to hit you; I am so sorry! All I could do was steer away from the gas tank. That's all the control I had!"*

My mind was in a brain fog. I heard him, but I didn't hear him. The truck driver had already called the police. I was not in pain. In fact, I didn't realize I had been hit, until I climbed out of my car and saw my back end was crushed into my back window. Looking at the driver and my car, I felt sorry for him, because he was so worried about me.

*"I'm fine. Thanks for not hitting my gas tank!"* I jokingly said, trying to let him know he didn't have to worry about me. We talked with the police officer and exchanged insurance information and went on our way. My boss could not believe I was at work after seeing the damages to my car. I actually did a whole day's work with no problems. After work, I picked up my children and went home. While driving, my mind began to realize that I could have been blown up had he hit my gas tank. My children would not have had a mom. My eyes watered as I realized they could have been left all alone.

On the third day, my speech impaired, making me sound like I had a foreign accent. I began to have blackouts, memory losses, and severe back pain. Instead of walking a straight line, I literally was walking in somewhat a slanted line, which caused me to walk into walls. These issues put me in the hospital and baffled the physicians, because they could not come up with a diagnosis for my problems. Their only conclusion was my body is reacting to a severe whiplash. After four months passed, I still had no improvement and the doctors did not feel I should go home.

I had to go home; my youngest son made it obvious my absence was taking a serious toll on him. Against my doctor's advice, I signed myself out of the hospital. The last thing I remember him saying was that I would be on muscle relaxers for the rest of my life, because they were the only thing keeping the nerves from tightening up the muscles in my back. Those muscle relaxers were literally taking my life. I was barely able to be present for my children, as the medication made me feel like a zombie. Often times, I felt like I was going to die, because many nights my breathing would just stop. One night, after my sons were sleeping in bed, I got down on my knees and prayed to God to help me be there for my sons; to give me all that they needed from me as their mother and to make them wonderful people. I cried like a baby that night as I laid in my famous fetal position.

The next morning, I heard God tell me to pick up my bed and walk. I stopped taking the muscle relaxers, which allowed me to become more conscious of what was going on throughout the day. Eventually, I was back to myself and in a better state of mind. God answered my prayer, He allowed for my sons to have a mother; a mother who was able to be there for them in a very powerful and positive way. Both my sons, Robert III and Marcus graduated from high school and became wonderful, confident, loving, responsible men.

I will forever be indebted to God for allowing me to have my mother in my life and for my sons to have me in their lives. Thank you Lord! He gave me *unmerited favor and divine provision.* Thank you!

**Linda Diane Wattley** is a published writer who began her first work of art with poetry. The poem, "I Wish" appeared in the Poetry Gem of the American Poets Society. For over twelve years she had her own religious/philosophical column in the Frost Illustrated Newspaper titled "The Best Will Show Themselves".

Today, God has awakened her to a new and extremely important message to share with the world. We must become more conscious of PTSD, Post-Traumatic Stress Disorder; she is presenting her newest work: "Soldier with a Backpack, Living and Dying Simultaneously". This work reveals the reality of the impact this disorder has on our veterans and civilian people's lives. It takes you deep within the soul of the inner dynamics of this disorder. Stress and trauma is guiding us farther away from love. Truth and understanding will guide us back to self-love and love for our fellowman.

## HE LOVES ME
### LETISHA GALLOWAY

In a world filled with advertisements and lives that look glamorous, it is easy to get swept up in it. Society tells us that we should have the latest fashion, car, and other items. Wanting and working for nice things is not bad. However, when you allow the things to control who you are, and to form your opinion of God, there becomes a serious problem.

There is a generation that is called the entitlement generation. The entitlement generation consists of those born between 1979 -1994. This generation believes that they are owed all of the great things that life has to offer; without an explanation of why they feel that way or working for what they want. They feel as though they should be given the highest salary possible and working their way up the career ladder is not included in their goals. Some feel as though they should have the position equal to or above their supervisor.

They may expect weeks of vacation time and to work when they want and get paid regardless. This entitled generation (not everyone) has a sense of ungratefulness for anything that is given, because they feel it is deserved. The same is true for some Christians today. Some have a sense of entitlement. Some feel as though, just because God created them, He is supposed to give them everything immediately. It doesn't quite work that way. Nowhere in the bible will you find that GOD said, *I created you, and at a snap of a finger, you will have everything you want.* God does not warm up blessings in the microwave and we have them thirty seconds later. HE is a God of order. He will never give us something that He knows we are not ready for; for some, this is hard to accept.

No one has the right to tell God what HE must do, what way to do it, and when to get it finished. None is more knowledgeable than God, for HE is all knowing. When God does things for us, it should be received with a grateful heart. One should never be so arrogant as to think they are the only one that God is concerned with and the only one who will get favor.

Furthermore, God is not going to give all of the favor to you either. HE loves everyone the same. One person can never be loved more than the other. God simply does not operate that way. HE's not sitting on the throne, *looking down saying, "I love him, she's ok, well he's not that great, and I should have created that one differently."* No, God created us all just the way He intended.

You may be asking me, *"How is that possible, when some have deformities?"* I'm glad you asked.

I was born with deformed legs. My legs were amputated above the knee when I was a baby. Now you may wonder how having my legs amputated is favor. When I went to the children's hospital for appointments, I saw children who were very ill. I saw children with legs and arms amputated. There were children with cancer and children who were too weak to get out of bed.

I'm not saying that God loved me more than them. I will say, that what went on while I was in the womb, could have caused things to be a lot worse than me having my legs amputated. As a small child, I didn't understand that favor was upon my life. I was simply a happy child. Some doubted my ability to function in school.

I can't take any credit. God showed them.

In school, some were ready to give up on me. My reading comprehension was lower than most children. There were two groups. The Blue Jays had me and another student. The Red Robins had the rest of the class. Some of the other children mocked us for being in the "slower" group as they called it. Throughout school, I struggled with math. I was told very early on that I was not college material. I didn't understand, given that I made the honor roll three out of four years in high school. I was disappointed. I started to lose any hope of attending college. My spirit was low.

Just when I was about to lose all hope, wonderful things began to happen. I was admitted to community college with financial help and scholarships. I received three outside scholarships from organizations. I didn't realize it at the time, but it was favor. God saw what I needed and came through. Not only did HE show up, HE showed out. I didn't have to spend a single penny for my education. I watched as others struggled to pay for college and I felt blessed. At that young age, I didn't understand the concept of unmerited favor.

I, like many others in my generation, thought that God handed out favor like cookies. If you're good, hold out your hand, and you get a treat. I truly didn't get it. I didn't realize that God doesn't have to give us favor; because HE's God and HE can do what He wants.

My first few months at community college started out well. However, later that year, I was suspended from financial aid. I stopped going to class. Along the way, I stopped believing in myself, so I simply stopped going. Two years later, I didn't know it, but God wasn't finished with me.

After I arrived in my new State, I stopped by the local community college. At first, I was afraid, but I kept having this feeling of urgency. I grabbed an application and filled it out in faith. I stopped by the financial aid office and told them that I would like to go to school, but had been suspended from financial aid at my previous college. The financial aid advisor said that she would help me. She said that it was time for a new start. I began to cry and thank her. She gave me an appointment to come back and fill out paperwork.

Here I was, a person who had previously thrown away her education, yet getting a second chance. That was favor. I was told at my other community college that I would have to come out of pocket for school, because no other school would offer me the option of federal aid or scholarships based on my track record.

They were wrong.

God had the final say in the situation. Not only did I get financial aid back, I received a work study position that helped to build my resume. Thanks to God, I finished community college cum laude, and subsequently finished my bachelor's degree.

After I graduated with my bachelor's degree, I became discouraged. Here I was with a bachelor's degree, working in retail. There is nothing wrong with working in retail, but that's not what I went to school for; I wanted to work in criminal justice in some way. I kept working and talking to God, asking HIM why I was in my seventh retail job, when I heard 'wait' in my spirit. A year later, I enrolled in a master's degree program. I did well. I was happy about my progress. Near the end of the program, my car broke down. I needed my car, because the bus didn't run all of the times I needed to get to class. School was forty minutes away in another county at the graduate center.

One day I was waiting for the bus, and one of my classmates asked me how I was getting to class for the weekend, because we had an accelerated class for two weekends. I told her of my plans to call for a taxi to take me home on Saturday and for one to take me all day Sunday. She told me that I didn't have to do that and she picked me up that weekend. Instead of spending $300.00 that weekend for transportation, I gave her $30.00 for gas and tolls. Not only did she give me a ride that weekend, she and I traveled together for the rest of our master's degree program and became friends. I finished my master's degree program Administration of Human Services with honors. I was ready to enter the work force.

Following graduate school, I applied for many State jobs, but I was never called. So, I accepted a part time job at a homeless shelter. It wasn't what I wanted, but it was in my field. I did the best job I could while I was there, which was three months, before I got called for a State job with Social Services. It was a seasonal social worker/case manager position an hour away, but I was happy to get the offer.

Ten months later, I applied for a seasonal senior social worker/case manager role an hour drive downstate. I was happy to be offered the position because, of course, it meant more money and the people in the office were nice. I knew some of them from new worker training. While I was there, I shared with a coworker that I would be applying for a merit job in the city I lived in. She stated that it wouldn't be likely I would get the job, because most people stay in seasonal positions for years. She told me that she was a seasonal for many years. I told her no offense intended, but that wouldn't be my testimony. She told me not to get my hopes up. I listened, yet I let it go in one ear and out the other that day.

A month later I got a call for an interview in the town where I lived. One of the supervisors I had previously met, told me that no matter what I do, keep talking until they have to turn over the paper. I did just what she said and it worked. God made it happen and I was promoted again to a merit senior social worker/case manager position.

When I went back and told the worker that I got the position she had a look of shock on her face. Not only was the position in the city I lived in, it was also less than five minutes from my home. It is a blessing to wake up each morning and know that I don't have to hurry up like I used to . . . to drive an hour away to work. I don't deserve any of it but HE decided to make it happen anyway.

My life has been filled with favor. One day I sat down and thought back over my life and the times that God showed me favor. I realized that I hadn't always said, "thank you." I didn't always appreciate God the way I was supposed to. I took his love and favor for granted; expecting HIM to do great things in my life, because when I was younger I thought it was His job to do nice things.

It is deeper than that.

God doesn't want people who are after HIM just for what they can gain. Now, when I pray, I first spend time thanking God for who HE is, and then made my request known; sometimes I don't even ask for anything. I just thank HIM. HE shows me favor, because I give Him the glory.

Today, the little girl who many didn't think would make it has four master's degrees. I only intended to get a second one, but I was told that I'd completed three at one time with a GPA of 3.86. I was shocked, because a staff person told me two years ago, that it would be one degree with one major and two concentrations. All I could do was cry. God had once again given me so much more than I deserved. The little girl who had reading comprehension problems, now has 12 book projects that she has been a part of. Ten books reached best seller.

With God anything is possible. HE loves us and wants the best for us. If we give HIM complete control, HE will shower HIS favor upon us. Keep believing.

**Letisha Galloway** is from Woodstown, New Jersey and currently resides in Delaware. Letisha is an author, speaker, poet, and empowerment coach. She is signed with Imani Faith Publishing a division of Peace in the Storm Publishing. She is a contributing writer for Women Walking by Faith Magazine and Wisdom for Everyday Life Magazine.

Letisha empowers people to follow their God given destiny. She frequently through her various social media accounts and blog empowers people to get out of their comfort zones and chase after their destiny. She believes that everyone has a purpose. She believes that when a person finds what they love to do they have found their purpose.

Letisha is regularly involved in bringing awareness to domestic violence. Surviving domestic violence herself, Letisha is a strong advocate for change and protection for those who feel they have no voice. Letisha is involved in bringing awareness to child abuse.

Additionally, she advocates for ending hunger and homelessness. Letisha is the mother of one, a son Jordan who is resting peacefully in the arms of God.

She obtained a Bachelor of Science degree in Criminal Justice from Wilmington University. She obtained a Master of Science degree in Administration of Human Service and a Master of Science degree in Administration of Justice from Wilmington University.

Letisha is presently a Senior Social Worker/Case Manager in Delaware. She may be contacted through her website **www.letishagalloway.com.**

## UNMERITED FAVOR: A HEALING KEY
**MINISTER JEFFREY MOORE**

Dictionary.com defines Favor as: "Something done or granted out of goodwill, rather than from justice or for remuneration; a kind act, the state of being approved or held in regard, excessive kindness or unfair partiality; preferential treatment."

Finding favor means gaining approval, acceptance, or special benefits or blessings. There is also a close association among favor, grace and mercy. The favor that human beings receive from God is often extended in response to prayer or righteous living. Those whose walk is blameless, such as Noah or Moses (Gen. 6:8, Exod. 33: 12-13), receive favor and honor from the Lord (Psalm 84:11).

In October of 2015, after going through a period of solitude with God, I began moving closer to my vision and purpose with God. On October 21st, while in my personal prayer time with God, I asked him to remove any distractions, obstacles, anyone or anything not sent by HIM for the next season in my life; anything that would prevent me from fulfilling my full time ministry desires through him. 14 hours later I was called into the manager's office and told that I was being released from my position. I had been let go from positions before, however, this time was different. There was a peace about it. While talking with my manager and the representative from HR, that prayer that I prayed for 14 hours prior never crossed my mind. I simply told them that I knew God was doing something, I would be fine, and that God had a plan for my life.

As I walked out to my car, I looked up to the heavens and spoke to the atmosphere and declared, *"God I do not know what you want me to do but, I know you have a plan. You are going to have to reveal every step you want me to take in this season."* I instantly received a message on Facebook, which simply stated, "I have crazy airtime and incentives available when you are ready." I then spoke with my editor and told her what had happened.

We began talking and she said something that changed the direction of my path. She was excited and almost hysterical. I could not figure out why she was excited at the fact I had just lost my job. Her comment, *"Jeff, God has released you into full time ministry,"* shocked me. I had just prayed this prayer and HE was already answering it.

The very next day, I launched **Healing Keys Ministry** with $75, a Facebook Page, and a prayer. You see, God had placed people in my life earlier (unbeknownst to me), that would play a pivotal role in the launch and continuation of the ministry.

Over the next four weeks, God set in motion a series of events that is nothing less than His unmerited favor. On November

2nd, by faith, I began Healing Keys Radio. Through those first interviews, and God speaking during this time of worship and my growing closer and closer with Him, He began showing me that I would be moving. He opened new doors and I knew there was no way it wasn't him. Provision began flowing in from places I never would have dreamed of . . . I received a check for $1,290 and messages from people telling me how the radio ministry was blessing them.

Three short weeks into the radio program, God once again showed me the direction I needed to move in, that would once again take me to a deeper trust and dependence with Him. He had been speaking to my heart about a move from Oklahoma. I wasn't sure exactly where that would be, until a very close friend of mine, told me in a conversation where I would be moving. The day before Thanksgiving, God caused events to unfold and showed me that I would be moving to Orlando, Florida. In a total act of faith, I bought a one way plane ticket and left everything I knew; my family and belongings… and moved.

After getting settled in Orlando, God once again spoke to me to launch a radio network, and a few short days later Praise Orlando Radio was born. Through faith, sacrifice and continually praying, worshiping and walking in the direction He directs me, there has been dynamic growth.

God aligns us with what (and who) is necessary to fulfil His purpose in our lives. I have had the opportunity to connect and become friends with so many brothers and sisters in Christ to expand the Kingdom, but more importantly, build relationships and help elevate the Kingdom; Gospel artists, authors, coaches, speakers - just "every day folks" with a testimony and love for God. All of these connections help me in my daily walk with HIM. When we walk with God, and align ourselves with Him, we transform from Grace to Favor. Through God's favor, I have received unmerited provision . . . deserving none of this, but through His love, He continues to give us favor and provision.

The beautiful part of all this is God's favor. I could not do any of this without His divine provision. I have not worked a corporate job since October 2015, and have not lacked. I have had a place to sleep, food in my stomach, and clothes on my back ever since I said "Yes" to His call.

As we go through every step of the process and draw closer to Him, and as we depend on Him more or trust Him more, HE provides.

It's not easy; I am not telling you to move States, or even to quit your job. However, I am telling you that He will provide for you. He will guide you. He will direct you. As long as you are obedient to His call, walking with him, and leaning towards Him every day of your life, HE will provide for you. There will be struggles. There will be a cost. The enemy will try and distract you. The enemy will send those to destroy you and God's plans for your life. Stay strong, stay encouraged, and don't give up. Only God can define you, and only God can take you further than you can ever imagine.

I am about to embark upon the next season or elevation that God has in store for me, which will require more dependence, more faithfulness, more trust and sacrifice, yet will undoubtedly be filled with more and more of His divine favor.

God requires sacrifices to make atonement and restore His favor, because of sin. In the Old Testament animal sacrifices were presented at the sanctuary with the hope that God would accept them and forgive the sins of the person making the offering (LEV. 1:3-4). Such acceptance was not automatic; however, the sinner had to have an attitude of repentance and humility (Gen 4:4-5, Micah 6:7-8). When Christ died on Calvary, the perfect sacrifice was presented, making it possible for all who believe to enjoy God's unmerited favor and divine provision (2 Cor. 6:2).

You see, God doesn't bless us because we deserve it. Honestly, we don't deserve it. God blesses us because of who HE is and HIS love for each of us. When we walk in obedience, continually striving for the closeness He desires, HE shows up! When we do our part, He is faithful and fulfills His promises to us. We live under grace when we first surrender our lives to Him but, there is much more. When we begin to walk in His ordained destiny for us, we begin to see a shift; a shift that takes us from living in His Grace to adding His favor!

There is a difference between grace and favor and once you see that shift in your life, you will not want to take a step back. Just your single act of obedience unlocks a treasure-trove of unmerited favor and divine provision in your life.

**Jeffrey S. Moore** grew up in Oklahoma City, OK and currently lives in Florida. He is the founder of **Healing Keys Ministry**, which has the divine purpose of reaching those who have experienced life challenges and helping them to heal and find their God ordained destiny. Healing Keys Ministry has numerous outreach ministries within its organization; including, **Praise Orlando Radio Network** and **Healing Keys Radio.**

Jeffrey enjoys being outdoors and spending time with family and friends, and continues to pursue God's calling, by devoting his life to Christ, and embracing everything God has in store for him.

For more information, visit **www.healingkeysministry.com**

## WALKING IN FANTASTIC FAVOR
**ALMENA MAYES**

**Favor ain't fair!**

I had heard this saying my whole life from the Christians in my church, whenever God did something for them. When something unexpected happened in their favor, even when it seemed that they were out of order with God, this phrase seemed a little like a "na na na na na" to those who did not seem to be as blessed.

I never quite understood favor. Did that mean you were God's favorite, and no matter what you did, He would bless you? Or, did it mean that on any given day, anyone could receive a blessing they didn't seem to deserve, based on their actions or character? It wasn't until God showed me, personally, what it meant to be favored, that I completely understood how spiritually fulfilling being in the favor of God could be!

I thought that I never wanted to have children. I wanted a fabulous career that allowed me to travel and party and become wealthy. I had no intention of being tied down. I did not want to be responsible for anyone else. I had a "me" mindset. God had already spoken to me and told me that He expected me to become a minister of the Gospel and to preach

His word, but that did not fit into my life plan. I thought I knew what was better for me than God, my Creator, did. How incredibly dumb was I? How can the pot tell the Potter how it should be used?

I went to college with the idea that I would finish early, go to law school, and then begin my life doing the things I wanted to do. In my effort to be "grown", I found myself pregnant and unmarried. I thought this was the worst thing that could have ever happened to me! Not only would I have to tell my parents that I was having a baby, but also, I had to rethink my plans for my own life.

**You see, God had a plan for me that I could not see!**

I went through the gambit of emotions. I was happy then sad; excited, and then frightened. Should I tell anyone? Should I just disappear? How could I face the baby's father with this news; our relationship was already shaky. I had been considering ending it, and I was sure he felt the same way. What about my parents? They were going to be very disappointed in me. My church, I was a youth leader, the choir director, and an example for other young women.

How could I go to them and say, that through pre-marital sex and personal irresponsibility, I had become an unwed mother? I felt as if my life was over!

**It ain't over until God says it's over!**

I went to my boyfriend and told him I was pregnant. His initial response was to question whether or not the child was his. This hurt me to my core; however, in retrospect, it really was a legitimate question. He and I had been in different cities for months and both of us were doubting the sustainability of our relationship.

Then came the task of breaking the news to our parents. We sought the counsel of our pastor in confidence. He, in turn, betrayed that confidence and told my boyfriend's parents before we had the opportunity to do so. To say all Hell broke loose would be an understatement. His parents told my parents and from there the war between the families began.

In addition, the church where I had served my whole life, suddenly became a place where I was no longer welcomed. They rallied around him, but treated me like trash to be cast out. I felt branded and labeled. Eventually, we decided to marry. We married for all of the wrong reasons, and it failed miserably; neither of us ready to be married or prepared to be parents.

**God prepares you for the challenges you will face.**

Our marriage was riddled with anger, betrayal and violence. Both of us did unspeakably hurtful things to each other. There was abuse and infidelity. There were financial issues and deferred educational aspirations; which caused resentment.

In the midst of all of this, we had our daughter. A beautiful, freckled faced, hazel eyed little girl came into the world unaware of the mess that she had been born into. We both loved her dearly, but that was not enough to hold our marriage together.

The only thing worse than the marriage, was the divorce. People outside of our marriage began taking sides, spreading rumors, and doing all they could to gain support for their point of view. No one wanted to accept the blame for the failure of this marriage and we weren't mature enough to control what was going on. It ended, just as it began, in a whirl of confusion and chaos.

There were times I thought I wouldn't survive the onslaught of hatred, and all it would take, to now raise a child alone. I was working, going to school, and trying to be a good mother. Still, I was unsure if I was truly capable of doing any of it, and worrying if I would ever be reconciled with God.

**Even if you veer off course, God does not change the plan.**

I had begun to believe that I was worthless. I looked at my life, and the life I offered my daughter, and I felt like a failure. When you have these grandiose dreams and you can no longer see a path to achieving them, it can be emotionally devastating. I watched all my friends graduate and move into their careers. They were progressing and growing and I was stagnant. I married again, had two more children, and divorced again. I couldn't understand why I just couldn't get it right. Why was success avoiding me? Why was I the only one who couldn't get ahead? I began to wonder if God had forgotten me. Had I strayed so far from the vision He had for me, that He no longer wanted me? I couldn't hear His voice. I started to believe that He was no longer speaking. The fact is, God was still speaking; I had just forgotten how to listen. I had become so engulfed in my own journey that I stopped listening for His guidance.

I hadn't only closed my ears to God, but I had also closed my heart. I had allowed my own feelings of failure to convince me that I was no longer worthy to be deemed God's daughter. I had to begin listening to the voice of God again. Suddenly, God's wisdom and favor began to impact my life.

God will re-energize your emotional and spiritual being when you open yourself up to receive it. The Bible says that "those who seek the Lord lack no good thing."

This is very true. The moment I turned to God and asked Him for His guidance, accepted His chastisement, and surrendered my life back into His hands, He began to bless me abundantly. I was able to return to college and graduate with my Bachelors of Arts. I raised my children and all of them are strong, resilient, and moral young people.

Finally, God is using me and all of my experiences to minister to people all over the world. You see, His favor brought me to my destiny! Here is the amazing thing, the path that He laid out for me will allow me to travel, fellowship with people from all nations, and earn a living doing what I love! Even through all my mess, His unmerited favor joined my desire with His purpose and has blessed me to live His promise.

I give all honor and glory to God.

**FAVOR AIN'T FAIR, but it is fantastic!**

**Almena L. Mayes** Almena L. Mayes is an associate minister at Coley Springs Missionary Baptist Church in Warrenton, N.C. She is currently serving under watch care at the Dream Center in Atlanta, Georgia. Born in Paterson N.J and raised in Warrenton, NC she sees herself as a city girl living a country girl's life. She is the mother of three beautiful adults and has three wonderful grandchildren.

Mena, as she is called by friends and family, attended North Carolina Agricultural and Technical State University where she studied Communications and Guilford College where she earned a degree in English with a concentration in writing.

In addition to writing, Mena is a singer and songwriter. She truly believes that God's message may be packaged differently for different people but the message is always the same; He saves, He heals and he restores.

Practical application of spiritual principles is Mena's mission in life. *"If we can't make the message relevant then people will not embrace it."* She feels a responsibility to present the message of God's never ending love to all people in a judgement free zone. "We all have issues, we all have problems but by being transparent to ourselves and to God we can grow beyond them."

She is an author, radio host, motivational speaker, and lifelong cheerleader. Her freshman book, Just Eat the Beans was released in January 2016.

Contact Almena @ **www.facebook.com/JustEattheBeans2016**

## LEVI'S TESTIMONY
**PASTOR KEVIN & LADY ARIANE WEBB**

We believe our lives consist of a series of moments; whether extraordinary or insignificant, they are woven together to create a fabric-like existence. Challenges, big and small, pierce our lives as needles interlace thread; fabricating unique patterns and strengthening the composition.

Like a beautifully constructed textile, our lives are meant to serve as a testament to the skill, power, and overwhelming awesomeness of our designer, our Creator. To ensure our Lord is given full credit for His "designs", we share these moments, or testimonies, with others in the hope of expanding His remarkable "collection."

Our testimony of God's awesome ability to weave a captivating moment of healing from the painful threads of fear and confusion, involves our twin sons, Luke and Levi. In hindsight, we should have known God would sketch a wonderful design through their lives, as they were born on Christmas Day. In the first hour of their birth, as they lay together in their crib, Levi's complexion was pale and his breathing irregular. He was almost taken to the Neonatal Intensive Care Unit (NICU) for further evaluation, but they discovered Levi had not taken a full breath when leaving the womb, and required incubation to gain lung strength.

Upon suggestion from the lead physician, Levi was placed on his stomach, and began to breathe easier. Despite being born five weeks early, and constant murmurings from hospital staff that they would likely need to remain for further observation after our formal discharge from the hospital, Luke and Levi came home to begin life with their siblings only three days after entering this world. They were welcomed by their beautiful older sisters, Laurin and Lindsey, and their beloved big brother, Shaun.

Luke and Levi were happy, precocious little boys with distinct personalities. Luke was affectionate, loving and enjoyed the closeness of family, while Levi was a born adventurer; always interested in climbing out of his crib and exploring his sibling's toys. At the age of two years, we noticed a swollen mass near Levi's thigh joint, and consulted his pediatrician. She assumed the swelling was a bruise that would soon heal. However, the mass only grew, and within a few months, our pediatrician referred us to a specialist for further evaluation.

After a few tests, we were told the mass would be "monitored" through quarterly visits, but there was no need for immediate concern. We returned home, confident in the health of our child and hopeful that the mass would resolve itself.

Fashion enthusiasts and believers know that the most appealing designs are rarely simple; but involve higher thread counts, embroidery and the addition of adornments to the fabric, such as beads or sequins. These additions typically require manipulation of the fabric through the piece of the needle, or rending the fabric, to allow room for ornamentation. Like a quality piece of cloth, unique testimonies full of seemingly insurmountable challenges are more compelling. In these situations, God's omnipotence is that much more awesome and all-encompassing.

Within a few months, we were rushing to Wake Forest University Baptist Medical Center (WFUBMC); Levi had sustained a fever of 103 degrees over the past few days that could not be tempered with medicines, cold baths, or any other home remedies. Desperate for answers, we drove to WFUBMC and were immediately shown to a room in the emergency area. We do not remember his name, and can barely recall the features of his face. But, we will never forget the warmth and concern in his voice when he stated his desire to admit our son into WFUBMC's Brenners Children's Hospital, to run further tests; despite his inability to give a specific diagnosis. We will always be thankful he allowed the ultimate Physician, and not years of medical training, to guide his decision.

Levi was taken to a room, and after a full day of testing, was initially diagnosed with a tumor. The mass near Levi's thigh joint had grown into a Nerf football-sized growth that was pressing into nearby lymph nodes, resulting in the high fever. Our medical team was led by a respected pediatric surgeon who had successfully performed this surgery in numerous children. However, we were more impressed by his gentle bedside manner, his willingness to explain every step of the process thoroughly, his penchant for bowties, and his request to pray with us before he entered the examination room.

**Pastor Webb Speaks:**

"As Levi was wheeled into the examination room, my knees weakened and I felt on the verge of collapse. I was surrounded by the love of family and friends; however, I wanted the cold metal of the surgical table, the intravenous needle in my vein and the knife pressing into my flesh. What I would have given to take my son's place in the operating room on that day! I felt out of control and anxious; concerned looks from my mother or sister led me to take refuge in a bathroom stall, where I cried and screamed into my balled fists or the folds of my shirt."

**The Testimony Continues:**

Eight excruciating hours later, our surgeon walked into the waiting area. He smiled and told us the tumor had been cleanly removed, despite having been attached to a portion of Levi's thigh bone and abdominal area. We left the waiting area to await the results of the pathology report and begin the recovery process with our boy.

Eight years later, we write this testimony, and fight back tears that we've shed often when thinking of this most profound moment that shaped the framework of our family fabric. The tumor was benign, and annual visits show no recurrence; however, one of the most amazing revelations was the birthmark located on Luke's torso that is the mirror image of the shape and location of the tumor removed from Levi. Every day is viewed as a blessing; every step taken with a leg muscle and every sit-up accomplished as testament to God's promise for Levi, and a reminder of His plan for our family.

**Pastor Kevin G. Webb** is the son of Deacon Freddie M. Webb and Cynthia R. Webb. Born in Charlotte, North Carolina and raised in Greensboro, North Carolina; he has one sibling Schala Harper (Ken) and is a graduate of James B. Dudley Senior High School. He attended North Carolina A&T State University where he joined Phi Beta Sigma Fraternity Inc., and later served during the Gulf War in the US Navy as a Submariner and Naval Diver for six years. In 2014, Pastor Webb graduated magna cum laude with a Bachelor of Arts in Ministry, minor in Leadership, from Carolina Christian College, in Winston-Salem, NC.

Pastor Webb was ordained through the Guilford Educational Missionary Baptist Association in February 2006, under the leadership of Pastor Darryl E. McConnell, of Faith Baptist Church in Gibsonville, NC. He is the founding pastor of Love Fellowship Believers (LFB) Inc., located in Greensboro, NC, where they "Desire To Fulfill God's Will" (Romans 12:1-2). Currently, Pastor Webb serves as a program mentor with PEAK Ministries' Journey Program, a discipleship ministry for high-school students attending Hope Academy in Greensboro, NC, and is the founding member and organizer of International Ministries United (IMU), a non-profit conglomerate of local ministries. Professionally, Pastor Webb is employed as Network Security Administrator for Guilford County government. You can connect with Love Fellowship Believers at: **www.lfbelievers.org**

## WHERE DO I BEGIN?
**MINISTER ELAINE MONTFORD**

Unmerited Favor and Provision - I scarcely know how to adequately explain, describe or define the depth or expanse of it, as it relates to me; but I can readily testify that I am definitely a recipient of it!

Oh yes, I know how the dictionary/Wikipedia defines it; and I've read about it over and over again in the Bible - but to choose one experience that would sufficiently express how this wonderful gift has impacted my life, well... this is the matter of my current dilemma.

One of the most common definitions I hear or read in regard to Grace, Mercy and Favor are these:

**Grace** - God blessing us with what we did not earn/do not deserve

**Mercy** - God sparing us from justice that we do deserve

**Favor** - God giving us the ability to produce wealth

Like most of you, I could share countless personal experiences of God's unmerited favor and provision, because each and every day I am the recipient of it. From the time my eyes open each morning, until I close them in slumber, and until they're opened again with a new day's light, His graces saturate my every moment.

In fact, to be listed among those who have the distinct honor of sharing a portion of our stories here, is just one more shining example of God's continuing favor towards me. He could have chosen anyone else, yet He chose me. I openly, and without shame, confess that God is my Source. There may have been a time in my younger years, when I would have tried to take some credit; but God has allowed me to know that He is now, and has always been my Source and Strength.

I want to share a brief bit of my history with you; not in an attempt to evoke sympathy or sensationalize my story; but simply as a point of reference.

I have worked most of my life. Even as a preteen, I did babysitting as a source of income, and as a teen, I worked at a daycare after school. So, when, as a single/divorced parent, at the age of 38, I had to leave my job in the medical field due to serious health issues, I was devastated. At this point, there was no mystery as to who my Source was. Let me share with you a few examples of His unmerited favor and provision in my life:

**GRACE**
On one particular occasion, I received a call late one Saturday afternoon, from one of the other ministers at the Church I attend, saying that one of our brothers in ministry was dealing with the death of a sibling; and as is our custom, the ministerial

staff was planning to present him with a love offering the next day. Well, it was several days before I expected to see a deposit of funds, and I only had $10. I didn't discuss my financial situation with the caller, I simply responded, "Okay Sis" and I hung up (and prayed about it).

I went to a Service later that (Saturday) night at another Church, and when it was offering time, I prayed for direction in giving. I gave $5.00, which left me with $5.00. The next morning I attended 8 A.M. Service at my Church, and again at offering time I prayed for direction. I knew if I gave my last $5.00 in the offering, I would have nothing to contribute to the love gift for my brother. God said, "Trust me . . . give your offering." I did as I was instructed. I was fully prepared to go to the sister who had called the day before, and explain that I had a heart to contribute, but just did not have the ready resources at that time.

After Service ended, and I was exiting the pew, a young lady approached me smiling, with her arms extended, to give me a hug. Now I knew that she was a member, and she would regularly greet me in this manner, but we were not really familiar, or close with each other outside of that. As she embraced me, she whispered in my ear, "Open your hand." She slid some money in my hand and turned and walked away. I began to shed tears of joy, without even knowing how much she had given, because I knew God had just answered my prayer!

As I stopped to put this gift in my wallet, I realized she had blessed me with five $20 bills. I went back to her (still with tears in my eyes) and thanked and hugged her again. She said, "I am only being obedient to what God told me to do."

She had no way of knowing the prayers I had prayed; but God did, and He used her as the vessel to channel that blessing through. Not only was I able to contribute to the love offering, I had enough to sustain me until that which I was anticipating, arrived.

I am grateful for Grace; but sometimes Mercy is more suitable to my case...

**MERCY**
Because of a series of ongoing medical issues, it was necessary for me to seek continual care with several different specialists. Along with this care, came the astronomical medical bills. Some of these were in the hundreds of thousands of dollars; so even after my insurance paid their portion, it still left a huge amount to be paid by me.

I remember one day I arrived to receive what was essential life-prolonging treatment, and I was told by the patient account rep that I could not be seen until my balance was paid off. I tried to explain the necessity of the care, and that I was making regular monthly payments; and although she sympathized with me, she did not have the authority to change the company policy. When I reached my car, I sat and cried and prayed.

Once I composed myself, I drove home.

The next day, I received a call from a patient accounts supervisor who said my doctor had made a request that my case be reviewed and extra consideration be extended. Not only was I granted access to continued care; they actually wrote off a large portion of my balance. God had extended His mercy towards me, because that was a debt I had incurred; but He touched the hearts of the staff and a portion of my debt was cancelled.

My first testimony had to do with God's sustaining blessing of Grace to meet a specific need. My second testimony displayed God's Mercy. My final testimony is about God's Favor. The difference for me is the distinction between giving me a fish; and teaching me to fish.

**FAVOR**
I did not fully understand in 1998 when I was seemingly forced to retire early due to health reasons, that it was actually God setting the stage to propel me into the direction of my Destiny. Now almost twenty years later, I'm recognizing another level of God's Favor.

Over the years I've had ample opportunity to see God's sustaining grace, and His mercy operating in my circumstance; and I learned how to operate more effectively within the area of my gifts and talents. Now I see God's favor operating freely!
I understand that wealth is not just money; but it is also wisdom, knowledge and the opportunity to be fitly joined

together with other parts of His body, each joint supplying. From that time until now, God has introduced me to some awesome Kingdom connections!

Just recently, He's presented an opportunity for me to partner up with a wonderful mentor who has the love and patience to teach me how to skillfully perfect my gifts, so that they can be used more effectively in God's Kingdom. In turn, using these same skillful gifts, gives me the ability to produce/gain wealth; which gives me the resources needed to reach . . . touch . . . influence a greater territory for the Kingdom.

I am fully aware that it is not me, or my abilities that have caused me to grow and prosper; it is God's Grace, Mercy and Unmerited Favor that has set me in this place, in this season . . . and it is all for His glory!

*"A gift opens the way and ushers the giver into the presence of the great".* ~Proverbs 18:16 (NIV)

*"But remember the Lord your God, for it is he who gives you the ability to produce wealth, and so confirms his covenant which he swore to your ancestors, as it is today."* ~Deuteronomy 8:18 (NIV)

I carry many scars (some physical , some emotional, even some spiritual) and I was once ashamed of them, because at that time, I saw them only as constant reminders of all that I had gone through and the pain and heartaches associated with it.

But now I wear them proudly, as badges of honor, because they are evidence of battles fought and victories won!"

**Minister Elaine Roundtree Montford** is an Author/Poet. Author of The Birth of Victorious Destiny, contributing columnist of The Bridge Builder column for The Acts of Women Of Power Magazine, co-author with best seller author Elder Desiree Harris-Bonner of Christian fiction novel series Love Never Fails (book 1 to be released Summer 2016).

Minister Montford is a member of the ministerial support team of Hurst Chapel African Methodist Episcopal Church (Winter Haven, FL), charter member and Central FL Region Director for Women Of Power, Inc.

She can be contacted via email at **elaine.montford27@gmail.com** or www.facebook.com/elaineroundtreemontford

Visit her website at: **and www.victoriousdestiny.com**

## FROM A CRASH TO A CAUSE
**RONALD ZION ROSEBORO**

On March 13, 2015, time stood still, as I stood at the threshold between time and eternity. At 1:30 a.m., I was driving to a third shift interview at the FedEx facility in my city. It had been at least 20 years since I had worked third shift; however, having a need for a financial supplement will cause most to sacrifice just to acquire additional income.

While driving, I began to get sleepy. Realizing the dangers of falling asleep at the wheel, I quickly rolled down the window to allow the cool morning breeze to become my wind of vigilance. As I wrestled between alertness and fatigue, I found myself periodically swerving from one lane to the next. My last resort was to blast my stereo, only hoping that both wind and sound would keep me focused to arrive at my destination.

However, within moments, my car violently crashed into an object that I could not identify. In fact, I could not immediately see. I struggled to wipe a fountain of blood which poured from my head into my eyes. Gasping for breath, as if it were my last, pain seized my body from the inside out. My legs were pinned and I could not move, as the jagged fiberglass body of my car surrounded me like a tortilla shell. While still gasping for oxygen and feeling like I was drowning in my own blood, I used my glass-riddled hand to wipe away more blood from entering into my eyes.

But suddenly my fingertips felt sharp objects protruding from above my left eye and forehead, which were fragments of glass. As I opened my eyes the windshield was within inches from my face as blood continued to flow. "What did I hit?" I mentally asked. With the pain of 10,000 needles in my side and with the pressure of a pickup truck upon my chest, I began spitting out blood and broken pieces of what used to be my windshield.

And then I outwardly prayed, *"Father in Jesus name please forgive me of my sins. Please forgive me for not fulfilling the call on my life. Please don't let me die this way. Jesus please give me another chance to repay my vows of ministry to you. I repent. Please save me. Please help me."*

Immediately, I heard a voice behind me asking, *"Are you ok buddy?"* I responded, *"I can't breathe. I can't move."* He then replied, *"Just hold on. We're gonna have to cut you out, but we will get you out. Just stay with me."* With shortness of breath, I uttered, *"Ok. Please get me out."* I was in and out of consciousness due to the severe trauma my body had absorbed. I heard the voices of emergency teams giving instructions, working, and the screeching sounds of a chain saw slicing into the top of my car, and then I lost consciousness.

I regained consciousness in the ambulance when I was asked a series of questions. I can also remember the gurney ride into the trauma center. It is standard protocol for trauma units to allocate an anonymous name of the victim for their protection. I was given the name Trauma Nation. When I once again regained consciousness, I was in the ICU. I learned that when I fell asleep at the wheel, I had slammed into a parked energy truck, where the technicians were repairing a power line.

Fortunately, none of the workers were injured nor killed; however, I had sustained two broken ribs, a lacerated liver, a ruptured artery in my heart (which required an emergency surgical stent), facial lacerations, a cut on my right arm that reached my tricep muscle (which also required surgery), a broken tibia plateau, and knee damage to my ACL, SCL, and PCL.

I remained in the ICU for six days and then was taken to rehab, where I was released 18 days later. During my hospital stay, I had to learn how to use the restroom and dress myself from a debilitated position. My medication included morphine, oxycodone, muscle relaxers, Ibuprofen, and a daily shot to prevent blood clots. However, the severity of the crash evoked a new perspective of life and grace, when my oldest daughter showed me the aftermath of my car, which rested in the cemetery of a salvage yard. The car looked as if it were dropped from the Empire State building. The engine was completely dislodged and pushed into the dash of the car. My car seat was uprooted and slammed into the backseat. The hood and car doors seem to look like one complete sheet of riddled metal.

If a picture is worth a thousand words, then mine is worth more words than the U.S. National debt. From the edge of death, to multiple surgeries, pain medications, ICU, rehab, wheelchairs, crutches, and many months of physical therapy, to now . . . God's grace and favor has truly been unmerited toward me.

In my short earthly visit, I have been through more than the average man. Yet, God's love and loyalty has surpassed my love and loyalty towards Him by innumerable light years. The hospital gave me a significant name as "Trauma Nation". I view this name as being divinely inspired and prophetic. It speaks to my mantle and mandate to be a usable instrument for God to heal a nation from its trauma.

We ALL have had some kind of event or incident of trauma. Oftentimes our trauma lies submerged in the depths of our souls, only to surface to sabotage our purpose, while poisoning our own perception of ourselves.

I was given unmerited favor on 3/13/2015, and I do not plan to allow it to be squandered. There are countless people who are fatally killed in car accidents with much less impact and trauma than I endured. I am grateful to walk in the rain, smell the fragrance of spring flowers, inhale oxygen, and see the goodness of the Lord in the land of the living.

This was a crash, which propelled me to a cause, much greater than myself.

**Zion** is a best-selling author, public speaker, radio host, empowerment specialist, leadership trainer, workshop facilitator, freelance writer, speech writer, magazine and newspaper columnist, spoken word poet, and ambassador of the Risen Christ. His compassion and heart for people, especially those who have been incarcerated or formerly incarcerated is revealed through every endeavor he pursues. His desire is to see people succeed despite their sentences or mental imprisonments.

His best-selling book, **"Is There a Samson in You?"** addresses the issues men face and educates the women who love them.

He recently launched **The Freedom Project**, an initiative dedicated to serving and empowering the disenfranchised and those industries which require education to assist those requiring restoration.

He is committed to upholding the integrity and standard of empowerment writing and speaking, by equipping others to live a life of hope, healing, and freedom.

Zion is a graduate of Lee University with a Bachelor's degree in Christian Ministry with a concentration in Pastoral Ministry.

All of his books are available on Amazon.

Connect with him via his website: **www.zionpoeticpress.com; twitter/instagram @shamefreelife;** and Facebook: **www.facebook.com/ZionSpeakz.**

## UNMERITED FAVOR & DIVINE PROVISION OF THE FIRST KIND
### NELLIE A. WOSU

Unmerited Favor and Divine Provision is more than one can ever expect and more than anyone could ever earn. It is the Father reaching out to cover you after all. It is in fact, I believe, His good pleasure to do so for His children. This awesome display of love is a direct outpouring of love to show you internally just what love is.

With unmerited favor and divine provision, there is the distinct advantage that He has placed upon you. It's akin to being a friend to God; a man (or woman) after God's heart. It's Jesus' love being displayed on the Cross at Calvary for you and me, even. Yes, it's even for the Sinner, too. Everyone is in position to receive God's unmerited favor and divine provision.

I submit to you: *Nellie Anita.*

You wonder, "Who is Nellie Anita?" Sometimes, I've wondered the same to myself. That same unmerited favor that we're speaking of in this narrative is what has been the primary modus operandi that has been forging me ahead since at least the day before I can remember. That being said, is that it has always been existent for me, prior even to Him stepping out onto the void and saying, *"Let there be ..."*

In the formation of the being (You), of unmerited favor and divine provision in the life of Nellie Anita, whom He named, I believe God whispers our name into the person's heart of what we're to be named. Knowing who and who you belong to is essential. We are not of our own self. We are here for the good pleasure of Him for His glory. Our life is not our own. Not one single thread of it is. Yet, He has chosen us, and in that choosing, He's given us "free will". Imagine that, we belong to Him, yet at the same time we have been given a privilege to exercise this belonging to Him at will.

My Aunt said that I had not had the worse life, but that it had not been easy either. She said that about me when I was very young. Was that a prophecy about the life that would come? Even still, there He is throughout every difficulty, clouds and torrential weather of massive proportion, I still see Him; unmerited favor, yet again, constantly providing the provision when everything had gone below the zero. Divine Provision brought it up beyond par in one way or another.

We exist here, but we also exist somewhere else, and that somewhere else is inside of us in our hearts, individual and collective as well, and that's also where He resides, where He is there we are, too. We're seated with Him, as Jesus sits with the Father, so we sit with Them. The Holy Spirit that resides in us is always there with us... so it makes all the sense in the world that we always sit with Him, Them, The Holy Spirit.

The Divine Provision in this case, is that His provision keeps us from harm and danger and will do so throughout this life that we have come to know. If it had not been for the Lord, where would you and I be?

Think about your own life of unmerited favor and divine provision. You know exactly what I am speaking of. There have been gates you've deliberately entered and were totally lost, but you were found also. Weren't you? Now what would you call that?

You call it unmerited favor and divine provision.

Have you ever heard the scripture that says "Love covers a multitude of sin"? Well it's right there in 1 Peter 4:8 as such:

*And above all things have fervent love for one another, for "love will cover a multitude of sins."*

And again the scriptures say that *"Hatred stirs up strife, but love covers all sins"*. Notice the plurality of "sins". That is found in Provers 10:12.

Love (God) is always covering us, with His unmerited favor (whether we can see that or not is up to us, the receiver of this unmerited favor), the divine provisions existed from the beginning of time. He spoke the provision for us by providing the vegetation, the livestock, and the living waters; both figuratively and literally.

Even in our worst of trials and tribulations, we have been touched by the hem of His garment, and provided for. The Blood that was shed still covers and anoints us in protection, provision, peace, passion as well as compassion. Love is essential. It is life, it is breath, it is forgiving, and it never fails.

The question I want to know is this: "Will we love Him as He loves us"? Do we have the capacity to love Him like that? Or, do we feel that's too deep? Are we afraid to venture out into

Love Land? Love Land is everywhere you are and there is another being.

I had a broken heart; literally and figuratively, both my loving heart and my physical heart. Both were broken. Nellie Anita has had a broken heart. However, in both cases, the ultimate unmerited favor and divine provision was poured out upon her, before she even knew that the heart of heart would never be alone; no matter how far away she went, no matter how many people would shun her or speak nonsense about her. No matter how many misconstrued lies about her would be told, or what the "they" thought and pronounce as "Gospel" about her life. She was, and is, and will always be filled with the only Love that exists; the Love of God. She's gone beyond surface loving of "love one another" and when it gets too difficult to engage that type of love, she simply reminds her self and remembers how the Love of Him mended her broken heart, picked her up from the ashes, and formed her again beyond measure.

His unmerited favor and divine provision has extended and caused her heart to expand beyond the normal confines of what a human heart is to be in the physical body of you and me. What I mean is, that my physical heart was the size of a basketball in my chest (literally), and the Lord caused me to live as I died daily to the devastating effect of the heinous and debilitating disease called heart disease - Congestive Heart Failure to be correct. It was classified as "CHF Stage IV".

Essentially, end of the line, with 10% functionality left. But God is bigger than heart disease; He is bigger than heart failure. He will cause your broken heart to be mended. How do I know? He has mended beyond repair my broken hearts; physical, emotional and even at times spiritual too. He caused the love of the hem of His garment to touch me, even when I didn't know or have the strength to desire such. He knows what we have need of, even before we know to ask. That's where the "Divine Provision" is in place for all, equally, whether we believe it or not.

Let go, free fall into what your inheritance has provided for you all along. And, that is your gifting of unmerited favor and divine provision. We could never earn such beneficial goodness. Therefore, our LORD sent His only begotten Son to shed His most precious blood for our unmerited favor and divine provision, even as we shouted "Crucify Him, Crucify Him", He has not crucified us. He has provided His unmerited favor and divine provision in every step, breath and moment of our life and our life to come. He has provided all of this for us without our knowing.

Just as an expectant mother joyfully awaits the birth of her child, He waits for us to birth the realization that He joyfully is already there; and that too is unmerited favor. For what do we have to offer Him, the One who has given His all? What would we, or could we, provide to Him? I submit to you what we could provide to Him is our divine self, the giving away of same back to Him, Who is our unmerited favor and divine provision as is extoled in His word as such:

### Please read: Psalm 23

This Psalm reflects unmerited favor for all, equally. Likewise, as I pray the Truth of His glory, I know that when I pray, I will be heard. Would you like to be heard by someone and yet they don't hear or care to hear what you're saying? God hears us always in all ways. He is a discerner of the intent of our heart. Go ahead and seek the unmerited favor and divine provision in this manner as we've been instructed. He's waiting on us.

**Please read: Matthew 6: 9-14**

That heart disease that I spoke of is a thing of the past; it no longer exists, whether spiritually, physically or emotionally. He paid the price for me and I freely receive His unmerited favor and the divine provision. Whether I'm accepted by anyone is not important, as long as I am accepted by Him. He's taken me beyond the diagnosis and prognosis of living with heart disease. He has me where I need to be only and always, and that place is with Him... and Him, with me, in my heart that fills to over brimming with Love, His love, His life. There is no better gift of unmerited favor and divine provision than the understanding and acknowledgement that this unmerited favor and divine provision goes beyond the natural realm; it is spiritual always. Realize you're sitting with Royalty, the King of Kings, the Lord of Lords, and that is unfathomable for a person like Nellie Anita, but she graciously receives all that He has provided for her yesterday, today and beyond forevermore. She has run and told that! Won't you do the same about your situation?

I Am the Encouraging One On Any Given Day for His Glory. That's my unmerited favor and divine provision which I freely share with you, you and even you, too! Amen. Selah.

**Minister Nellie A. Wosu** is a National Spokesperson & Champion for WomenHeart: The National Coalition for Women with Heart Disease, the nation's only patient advocacy organization headquartered in Washington, DC. Nellie is also a patient spokesperson for national health agenda Measure Up Pressure Down.

Minister Wosu was referenced in an article in the March 2013 Edition of ESSENCE Magazine concerning the impact of stress upon today's woman. Also, in December 2012, Wosu penned her journey with heart disease entitled *"The Keeper of Me"* an Amazon Best Seller, published by **Gatmoon Publishing, L.L.C.** located in Concord, North Carolina of which she is the Publisher & CEO. She is the owner of NWN Radio & Television Broadcasting on the WWW streaming from SIBN.NET.

Minister Wosu is not only surviving with heart disease she is thriving and encourages others to do the same with their health journey. Nellie believes the disease has propelled her into her life's mission and purpose for His glory to benefit many perhaps even including you!

Contact her at **www.gatmoonpublishing.com**

# FAITH AND FAVOR
### ANGEL M. BARRINO

*"The Lord is my Shepherd; I Shall Not Want..."*

~Psalm 23:1

When I think of the words unmerited favor and divine provision, my heart becomes overwhelmed with emotion, since I have been the recipient of such provision the better part of my existence. Most of my adult and faith believing life, I have heard people recite these words, *"Favor ain't fair."* Now to know me is to know that I absolutely abhor clichés and this statement puzzled me for years. The Word of God declares that He will bestow favor upon His children and provide for them, so then why is favor unfair?

Just my deep thoughts.

Beginning this year, January 2016, I made a huge leap of faith. My life had been uneasy, because business seemed to be at a standstill. New clients were basically nowhere to be found, a few existing clients had abandoned me, and my personal financial life was a wreck. Searching for tranquility, I decided to leave my home town and journey to the big city of Atlanta.

For many years I had wanted to live there. Many told me the opportunities were vast. Inwardly, my spirit longed to know what it would be like to be in a place where I could grow in all areas of my life. My concern increased, however, as I had just met a wonderful gentleman, and begun a friendship which was growing into a beautiful relationship.

Having a long-distance relationship has never been my desire, yet we managed to make it work. A client friend had hired me to publish her freshman book and encouraged me to come there to work with her and bring the vision to pass. So what did I do? Left the small town and helped her bring her vision to pass.

Abba Father's provision and favor was amazing. For more than 30 days, I wanted for nothing. Connections were made in the job sector and life progressed. However, in February things shifted and I made a decision to move to Northern Georgia. A high school friend rented me a room in her home and again I wanted for nothing. For six months Abba Father provided for me in that place. It was as if I was the female version of Elijah (the 2016 version) when he was being fed by ravens at the brook. There was such a level of peace I had not known before.

Even though obstacles presented themselves, I had encountered the Shepherd of my soul in a new way – Psalm 23 had never been more real in my life. The Holy Spirit reminded me of every place in my journey where He was my provision, protector, and peace. He reminded me that He was still with me and I had nothing to fear. My companion and I continued praying each day for the Father's direction concerning my destination and journey. There were two very specific things I prayed years ago and I experienced the answer to both of those prayers during this season of my life – as if I were on a spiritual sabbatical and Yahweh needed me to be in a place where there were no real distractions. He has shown me His sovereignty and is leading me beside the still waters. He is restoring my soul.

Who does not want to serve a God like Yahweh? Like Abba Father, the King of Kings and Lord of Lords? The Great I am – the Creator of heaven and earth and every living thing? Serving Him with gladness and joy is my heart's desire. He loves me so much, that He took the time to teach me how to trust Him, by leading me into the desert place. He led me to an unfamiliar place to become more familiar with Him.

However, being led to Georgia is not the end of the story. As I type this, the story of Unmerited Favor and Divine Provision in my life is still being written. Angels on earth have been covering me, protecting me, and providing for me as He directs them to. It's unbelievable how I am living out the words Unmerited Favor and Divine Provision. When the Holy Spirit gave me this title, I had no idea what was about to transpire in my life.

Beyond measure, I am being provided for.

Business is growing and I have been hired by a client to handle her administration. Referrals are coming and I have been hired by two additional companies to oversee projects and handle their executive administration. The more my spirit, heart and soul (mind, will and emotions) become aligned with His Word or His will, the more He entrusts to my hands.

My mind and spirit understand that I had to be in a place to receive what He desired to produce in me and that was trust, ministry, forgiveness and restoration. In return, He provided for me.

Living out Psalm 23 is a prophetic blue print for those whom I come in contact with daily. Many need to know that Abba Father has not forsaken them, nor has He given up on the promises He made. In the last year, numerous believers have expressed their desire to throw in the towel, because the promises have yet to be seen, but I want to encourage you – Abba Father is faithful. His Word is truth and it will accomplish what He sent it to do. Let me empower you and minister to your soul – *favor is fair* and if you simply trust Him, and rely on Him completely, you will see just how equitable He is.

Your life may look like it is falling apart; however, in reality, it is falling together. Do not give up, out or in. He is with you always, even until the end of the earth. He will never leave you. He promised He would take care of His children.

Every day is a new day. Not sure what each day will bring, I put my life in His hands and ask for His direction. At no time has this been easy. It has been scary, yet He said, *"Fear not for I am with you."* His presence is with me at all times. My message to those of you reading this book is to simply give your all to Him. Can you trust Him? Can you allow Him to lead you into the deeper places within Him?

There is a worship song I love and the melody simply says, *"Spirit lead me where my trust is without borders, let me walk upon the waters, wherever you would call me."*[2]  Not only has Psalm 23 come alive within me, but this song resonated with me this entire year, as trusting Him is the lesson Abba Father is teaching me.

Allow me to encourage you once again - believe in Him and believe in His promises. Believe in the gifts He has placed within you. He will use them for His glory and He will divinely provide and give you unmerited favor. Surrender your will to His and watch Him move supernaturally and meet every need. Give Him your heart and allow Him to be everything you can imagine. He is sovereign, He is royalty, He is worthy ... He is our Father.

Embrace the words of Psalm 23. Internalize them. Visualize them. Pray them for yourself, over your household, family and community.  Write them forever into your heart and mind. Remind yourself of their truth and the love of our Father, which illuminates through them.  Speak them daily.  Believe them. They are light, truth and healthy to every aspect of your life:

*". . . He maketh me to lie down in green pastures: He leadeth me beside the still waters. He restoreth my soul: He leadeth me in the paths of righteousness for His name's sake. Yea, though I walk through the valley of the shadow of death, I will fear no evil: for thou art with me; thy rod and thy staff they comfort me. Thou prepares a table before me in the presence of mine enemies: thou anointest my head with oil; my cup runneth over.*

---

[2] From Oceans (Where Feet May Fail); by Hillsong United

*Surely goodness and mercy shall follow me all the days of my life: and I will dwell in the house of the Lord forever."* ~Psalm 23:2-6

**Angel M. Barrino** is a woman after God's heart who daily seeks direction concerning her purpose, assignments and businesses. She specializes in assisting authors and entrepreneurs by providing strategies and support which help them go to the next level. She has helped numerous authors become Best Sellers on Amazon, including herself, using her strategic and winning platform. She is the Managing Director of Angel B. Inspired Inc., the parent company for several businesses which include publishing, marketing, coaching. She is the former Sr. Editor for Simply Elevate Magazine since 2014 and Founder of The Praise Network Global. She serves as a personal and relationship coach for Relationship Tuesday on Help 4 Men Radio Network. She is also the visionary for Purpose and Praise Ministries, a ministry dedicated to restoration, forgiveness and reconciliation.

Her life's purpose is to help others utilize their gifts to create multiple streams of income, bless others and bring glory to the Lord. Her heart's desire is to always worship Abba Father through song and serving.

She is the author of *His Purpose, My Praise*, Co-creator of *Organized Obstacles: An Underdog Anthology*, *Book Marketing 101 with Angel B.* and *Becoming One Flesh: Marriage God's Way*.

You can find her books on Amazon.com as well as through her website at **www.angelbarrino.com.** You can also connect with her via Facebook: **www.facebook.com/AngelBarrino.angelbinspired,** Twitter/Instagram **@angelbinspired** and LinkedIn **at www.linkedin.com/in/angelbarrino.**

## Beloved Reader...

Thank you once again for sowing into this vision and the ministry of *The Praise Literary Collection*. Each author has poured out of their heart and shared the innermost part of themselves.

This is our prayer:

*Father we glorify and magnify you for this moment in time you have given each of us to share our gifts and insight with the world. We know that without you we are nothing. Our hearts, souls and spirits edify you for you are Sovereign. You have shown yourself mighty in our lives and we thank you for allowing us to impart what you have given us into the lives of others. As your Son prayed for his disciples in John 16, we pray for the readers who join their faith with ours and we ask that you protect them, enlarge their territories, increase their faith, and provide for them as you provide for the birds of the air and the fish of the sea. Show them a special sign of your favor and draw their hearts closer to you so that they may experience a deeper relationship with you because of these words. We thank you now for salvation and deliverance that will come to those who need it and restoration to those who seek it. You are our Shepherd and we thank you for being Abba Father.*

*Selah*

**PUBLISHER:**

**Angel B. Inspired Inc**.
P.O. Box 49647
Greensboro, NC 27419
(800) 378-4098 Ext 8
www.angelbarrino.com
www.angelbinspired.com
angelbinspired@gmail.com


Editing/Interior Illustration/Cover Design:
**DHBonner Virtual Solutions LLC**
www.dhbonner.net